Weardale Way

By the same author:
EBOR WAY
NIDDERDALE WAY
YOREDALE WAY

Weardale Way
A 78 mile walk following the River Wear from Monkwearmouth to Cowshill

by
J. K. E. Piggin

Dalesman Books
1984

The Dalesman Publishing Company Ltd.,
Clapham, via Lancaster, LA2 8EB

First published 1984
© J. K. E. Piggin 1984

ISBN: 0 85206 789 5

Printed by Alf Smith & Co., Bradford.

Contents

	Page
Foreword	7
Introduction	9
Monkwearmouth to Durham	15
Durham to Bishop Auckland	23
Bishop Auckland to Stanhope	28
Stanhope to St. John's Chapel	36
St. John's Chapel to Cowshill	42

Cover photograph of Daddry Shield, near Eastgate, by Geoffrey N. Wright.

Maps by the author and E. Jeffrey (page 29).

Drawings in the text by T. Brereton, Fred Lawson, Janet Rawlins, D. C. Smith and Alec E. F. Wright.

Foreword

WHEN I announced to some of my walking friends that I intended to spend a week of my summer holiday walking the length of the River Wear from Monkwearmouth to Cowshill their attitude towards me changed considerably, as it does when some poor soul is about to be committed to the mental hospital! Jocular Yorkshire remarks like "Bit mucky isn't it?", "Are there enough paths up there?", "Don't fall down the pit" and "Can you speak the language?", came like snow on the Himalayas and lasted until the eve of my departure.

When I returned fit and bronzed after a week in which the sun shone almost all the time, the scenery was better than I ever dreamed it would be and the inhabitants of the County of Durham had welcomed the "slightly eccentric" Yorkshireman with the haversack on his back. Wherever I went there was much to tell and of course a slight change in attitude.

Some two years later I had the opportunity to take many of those walkers on the route described in this guide and the transformation was complete. All enjoyed the walk tremendously, were as impressed as I had been with the scenery and last but by no means least the hospitality of those who went out of the way to help and encourage us as we passed across the county of which they are so rightly proud. Many of them voted this the best walk ever — not bad when it is appreciated that we have walked together for more than ten years and approximately two thousand miles!

Since then I have had the opportunity to meet and correspond with officers of the Councils, County, District and Parish; the Country Landowners' Association; National Farmers' Union and many other individuals, most of whom have shown a keen interest in the walk and I'm sure will do everything in their power to make your journey through the county a pleasant and enjoyable one. Providing of course that you respect the countryside in all its aspects — I'm sure you will.

Ken Piggin,
69 Beech Avenue, Holgate Road, York YO2 4JJ

Introduction

Durham County and the River Wear

Those whose only impression of the historic County of Durham has been obtained from the window of a high speed train speeding between Darlington and Newcastle can have little idea of the beauty of the county. They may have stopped for a few moments at Durham and admired its magnificent cathedral dominating the ancient city but the overall impression will be of an area struggling to recover from the scars of industrialization, a slow process in these days of industrial decline and shortage of funds. There is however a vast area of great natural beauty and many places of historic interest beyond the narrow confines of this industrial belt and by far the best way to find them is by putting on a pair of boots and exploring the many public footpaths and bridleways.

The 78 miles walk following the River Wear from Monkwearmouth to Cowshill described in this guide provides opportunities for walkers to visit and explore many of those places passing from east to west across the very heart of the county. First southward to the cathedral city from which it takes its name and onward to Bishop Auckland, the river then turns westward through the region known as "Weardale proper" to the source of the river under Killhope Law, a wild and remote region where the boundaries of Durham and Cumbria meet. The Way takes the walker past ancient castles, across the ancient and beautiful city of Durham, through delightful parkland and meadow, riverside paths and across moorland and fell to provide a walk of infinite variety which will suit walkers of all tastes.

The Walk

A 78 mile linear walk following the River Wear from Monkwearmouth to Cowshill, the paths are all public rights-of-way, most of which are frequently used and easy to follow. Consultation has taken place with County, District and Parish Councils, the Country Landowners' Association, National Farmers' Union and Ramblers' Association and it is hoped that most of the route will be waymarked in the near future.

Walkers are reminded that they are only entitled to walk the path and that the landowners' and farmers' right should be respected at all times. There are several places where the route passes close to isolated houses and farmsteads sometimes passing between farm buildings. Please do not loiter, there is nothing more distressing to a lady left on her own in a lonely place than to have suspicious

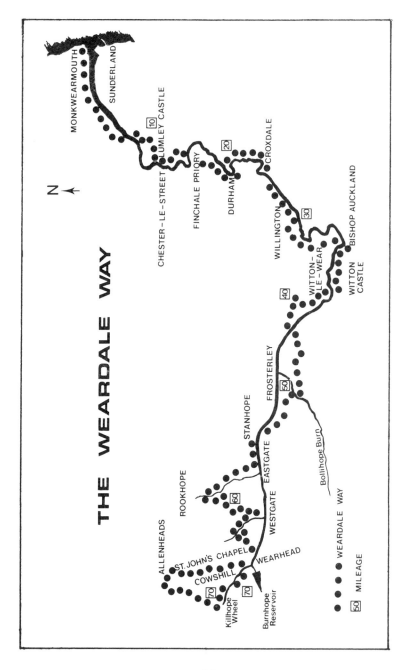

characters wandering about, or examining expensive farm machinery.

Please obey the Country Code at all times, walk in single file through growing crops and don't forget that this includes meadow land which predominates on this particular walk. Dogs should preferably be left at home but if this is not practicable should be kept on a lead at all times. In the lambing season sheep become restless even if they only scent the dog with possible harm to lambs and sheep — during lambing if you must take the dog try to avoid them by taking to the road.

Finally a word on the need for safety precautions in the high fells in West Durham where rain or snow falls on two-thirds of the days in the year and the weather can change dramatically in a few moments. Always go out well prepared with good strong boots, warm clothing and good quality waterproofs, make sure you have food and water for the day and emergency rations to keep you going for at least one more day, take a first aid kit, compass, whistle and torch and above all use common sense. There is an excellent leaflet setting out a code of practice for fell walkers called "Safety on the Durham Fells" which every walker along the Weardale Way should possess. Free copies can be obtained from the County Planning Department, County Hall, Durham DH1 5UF or the author — please enclose S.A.E.

Transport

The Way is adequately covered by public transport, both road and rail, the county being also blessed by two of the best timetables in the country. Detailing road and rail they cover the north and south of the county and provide a great deal more information on tourist offices, enquiry offices, market and early closing days, town maps, etc.

The guides are 30 pence each (plus 40p postage and packing on any quantity) and amendment leaflets which are published about four times a year are free. Order from County Planning Department, Bus and Train Guide Orders, County Hall, Durham DH1 5UF.

Badges and Completion Certificates

It is hoped to have badges and completion certificate available by the time this guide is published. Details will be supplied by the author on receipt of a stamped addressed envelope.

Maps

The directions given are fairly detailed but no one should set out on the walk armed only with this book. Words can be quite deceptive at times and quite small changes in the countryside can result in vastly different interpretations of the written word. It is essential therefore

to invest in a set of 1:50000 Ordnance Survey Maps but if you can possibly afford them obtain a set of 1:25000; they will make route finding so much easier and in this case not much more expensive.

Maps required

1:50000
Sheet 88 Tyneside
Sheet 93 Teesside and Darlington
Sheet 92 Barnard Castle and Richmond
Sheet 87 Hexham

1:25000
Sheet NZ 25/35 Chester-le-Street
Sheet NZ 24/34 Durham
Sheet NZ 23/33 Spennymoor
Sheet NZ 03/13 Crook
Sheet NY 83/93 Weardale
Sheet NY 84/94 Rookhope

Other Information

Those who would like more information about Weardale are advised to visit a Tourist Information Centre where there are many free leaflets produced by the County Council and Wear Valley District Council.

Useful Reading

Includes:
"Farming in Weardale"
"Five Weardale Walks"
"Walkabouts — Stanhope and Wolsingham"

Finally a few hints on how to help the farmers along the route:

1. Close **all** gates — do not assume that the farmer has left one open — it could be another walker in front of you. All farmers would prefer to open a gate rather than run the risk of having their stock stray.

2. In lambing time the farmers have to find all sorts of little dodges to keep the tiny animals fenced in. Help them by fastening a kissing gate if they have some method of fastening them and make sure that small wooden gates or other devices are replaced across stiles in stone walls.

3. Climbing gates should not be necessary but if it is always climb over one at a time at the heal (hinge) end. Climbing over anywhere else will put strain on the gate and consequent damage.

4. Always report straying cattle or cattle in difficulties to the nearest farm.

5. Similarly if you see broken fences or have the misfortune to break one make a temporary repair if you can and report it.

Monkwearmouth to Durham

AFTER leaving the North Sea on our journey westward to the source of the River Wear we soon come across a little jewel. The church of St. Peter, all that is left of the monastery of Monkwearmouth, was originated by a Northumbrian nobleman Benedict Biscop who had made several pilgrimages to Rome and finally returned to promote the christian faith in his own country. He employed builders from Gaul to build the first stone church on the site about AD 674, probably it is thought on the site of a previous Irish/Saxon monastery. It is believed that the original building was the first church in England to have glass in its windows and the barrel roof of the porch is said to be the only example of Saxon vaulting above ground in England.

Thus we begin our journey and although our path will go under and over great arterial roads, besides scenes of industrial activity and sadly to one or two places where the scars of the coal mining era still remain, they are just small irritations along a route which takes us through the heart of Durham County and some of the most beautiful countryside in England.

A little further along the road we find the Monkwearmouth Station Museum, a land transport museum in the former British Rail buildings. It is then out into open country to pass under the impressive modern structure which carries the A19 across the river on its way to Newcastle. A delightful wooded path along the riverside follows and before we realise it the Washington Wild Fowl Trust Refuge comes into view, 103 acres of lakes and landscaped grounds which thousands visit to view a comprehensive collection of the world's waterfowl.

Penshaw Hill and on top of it the Doric Temple which was erected by public subscription to the memory of the first Earl of Durham, John George Lambton, who died in 1840. The magnificent structure, which has eighteen hollow columns thirty five foot high, one of which contains a staircase on the roof, is now the property of the National Trust. Beyond Washington Staithes we get a close up view of another wonderful feat of engineering, Victoria Viaduct, so named because it was completed on the day of Queen Victoria's coronation, June 28th, 1838. Carrying the railway across the River Wear it is 270 yards long and nearly 150 feet above the river. The design was based on the pattern of Trajan's Bridge at Alcantara in Spain and built from grey stone quarried at nearby Penshaw.

Passing through Sir James Peel Park with its small lake and replica of the Earl of Durham's Memorial, we arrive at where over on the other side of the river behind the inn can be seen a memorial stone on top of a small hill. This mound is known as Worm Hill and is reported to be the hill which the legendary worm of Lambton coiled round to bask in the sun. Those who wish to know more will find the story in local history books but we must continue our journey through the impressive grounds of the Lambton estate.

The next section is one of the prettiest parts of the walk to Durham, passing along woodland paths with Lumley Park Burn splashing along the bottom of the ravine. Beyond the tiny village of Castle Dene the walk enters Lumley Park and another splendid woodland walk. This passes to the rear of Lumley Castle and along the east bank of the River Wear with splendid views of this great four square castle with the battlemented tower at each corner which dates from the end of the 14th century. It is noted as a conference venue and for the medieval banquets held there.

Our path lies along the east bank of the river but worthy of mention is the township on the other side, for Chester-le-Street in addition to being a useful place to find refreshments has a long history. A Roman station halfway between Vinerium (Binchester) and Aelius (Newcastle), it was also to the wooden cathedral there that the monks of Lindisfarne brought the body of St. Cuthbert when they fled from the Danes and there it rested until another Danish attack forced them to move it to Ripon. We must however continue our journey towards St. Cuthbert's final resting place in Durham Cathedral, but before arriving there we have a visit to make to what is without doubt the loveliest ruin in the county.

Finchale Priory (pronounced Finkle) lies in a secluded wooded site on a glorious bend of the river, by far the better approach being from the north. The steep and winding wooded walk down to the river rushing noisily over the rocks below is a delight in itself, but add to that the occasional glimpses through the foliage of the priory ruins standing in the well-kept lawns on the other bank and you get a picture of incredible beauty. The Finchale story starts with St. Godric, born in 1065, who became a sea captain and in 1102 made a pilgrimage to Compostellan in Spain. Later he resolved to leave all worldly affairs to become a hermit. Variously reported as being domiciled, if that is the word, at Lindisfarne, Carlisle and Wolsingham, he eventually came to Durham Priory and in 1100 was granted permission to live at Finchale where he built himself a turf-covered hut and a wooden chapel dedicated to St. Mary about a mile upstream from the present ruins. The priory eventually became a holiday retreat for monks from Durham but present-day walkers will probably be more interested in resting awhile in the cafe beside the ruin where you can be sure of a good cup of tea and home-made cakes during reasonable hours.

Refreshed we journey on past Her Majesty's Prison at Frankland

and before long we see ahead the great cathedral of Durham aptly described by J. S. Fletcher as "a great poem in stone, rising so proudly above the brown Wear". The nearer one gets to Durham City the more one appreciates the spectacle of cathedral and castle soaring high above the river — little wonder that tourists in their thousands come here to tread the path of the medieval pilgrim to the shrine of St. Cuthbert.

Route   19 miles

THE walk starts at the War Memorial near the coastguard station at Roker, at first in a southerly direction and then very quickly turning right along the road which goes alongside the river. For the next four miles the walk passes along the road in close proximity to the river, passing the ancient church of St. Peter on the left and Monkwearmouth station, now a museum, on the right and along the A1231. Just beyond the second roundabout along this road and where the riverside works give way to grass for the first time, the path goes to the left down to the riverside. Turn right along the river's edge and straight ahead to North Hylton, passing the public house and under the impressive new road bridge carrying the A108. Fork right down a lane but be careful, the footpath goes up the hill to th,e right opposite a house on the left, the way straight ahead being barred by a large gate.

Climb up the hill through the trees over a stile turning left along the edge of the wood. The path now gradually meanders down through the wood, a delightful path which runs along the river's edge and which will more than compensate for the rather tedious walk along the road. The path is very clear, making its way up through the wood again, skirting the edge of it and then turning left over a stream and just inside the wood to a stile. Before the stile turn left down a path which takes one down to the river's edge and over a stream. Approximately 150 yards past this spot there is a well established path which swings up to the right and then diagonally across the field with Low Barnston Farm on the right. Over a stile and a footbridge there is a footpath sign which indicates the path alongside the wire fence of the Wild Fowl Park. Continue past the entrance and swing left along the other fence with Penshaw Hill and the Earl of Durham's Monument straight ahead on the other side of the river.

Over a stile the path goes down to the river, turning right along the bank, over a stile and through some bushes to a wider track where there is another track going up to the right. Ignore that and turn left along the track which runs to the left of the huge mound of waste material, past a house and along the road for a short distance before crossing the footbridge over the Wear into Washington Staithes. The Way continues by turning right past some bungalows, over a stile and a very pleasant walk along the tree-lined banks of the Wear to the impressive structure of the Victoria Viaduct carrying the railway over the river.

Go straight ahead along the riverside path through Sir James Peel Park,

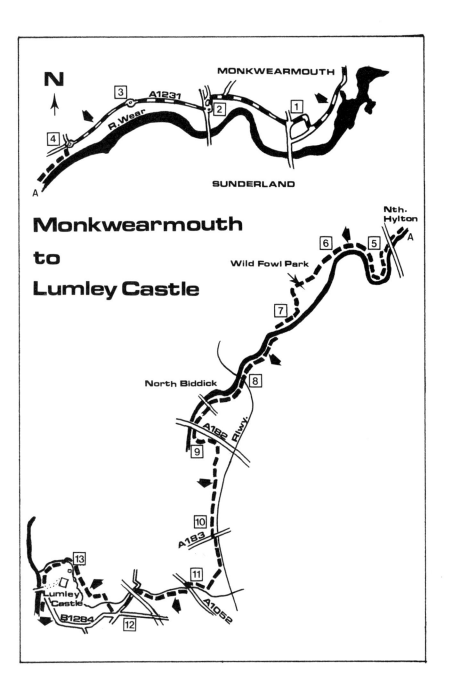

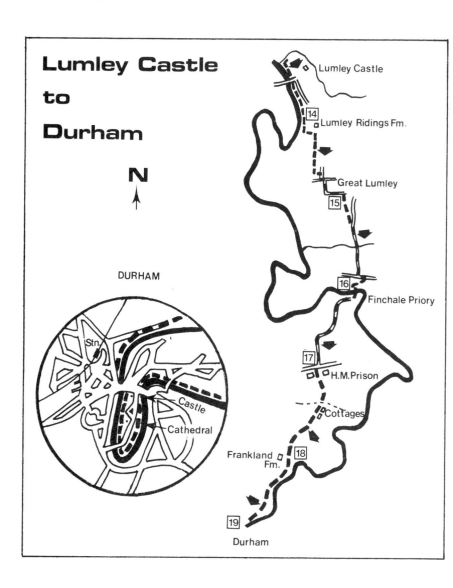

passing the lake and replica of the Earl of Durham's monument, and between cottages and river to the bridge where refreshments and perhaps a climb up Worm Hill can be enjoyed at the other side of the river. The Way however lies to the left along the road for a short distance before turning right down a concrete track. Go straight ahead at the end of this road along the clearly defined and signposted bridleway which goes under the road bridge, swings left away from the river and beside the motorway for a short distance, and then swings right into the Lambton Estate. Go straight ahead where lanes cross and along a very pleasant walk through the wood. This ends at a road where our route lies to the left for a short distance and over a stile on the right just before the railway bridge. The path is now clearly defined alongside the fence, with the coke works over the other side of the railway, over stiles and then swinging right up the old railway formation which leads straight into the outskirts of Bournmoor. Go straight ahead across the road and over a hill to a stream, turning right alongside it on a very nice walk past a few houses and through a wood to a bridge. Go over a stile, turn left over the bridge and then right over another stile and along a wonderful path through the woods with the Lumley Park Burn running through the gorge below. The path eventually goes down to the stream, past a waterfall and under the road bridge carrying the A1 where a few yards down the road the *Smiths Arms* provides sandwiches (not on Saturdays). Continue along the road for approximately 500 yards to the tiny village of Castle Dene where the path is to be found down a lane on the right between the houses.

A footpath sign indicates the way but be careful not to follow the track which swings left. Keep straight ahead through the wood and over the stream, turning left at the edge of the wood along another delightful wooded walk which eventually passes to the right of the Garden House. About 500 yards past the house the path turns left over a stream to join the riverside path. This is a very pleasant walk along the river bank past the entrance to Lumley Castle, keeping to the same side of the river at the bridge and with the golf course to the left. Half a mile beyond the river bridge there are two stiles and a small bridge over a stream. Pass over these and continue along the path up through the trees beside the river and then along the field boundary, turning left along the edge of the field, through a stile and immediately right through another one to proceed along a good path along the left-hand side of a hedge. To the left the walker will see Greater Lumley village across the field and when opposite the tiny church the path turns left to emerge into the village at the cross roads. Go across the road from a bus shelter, turn left and then almost immediately right along a new housing estate with houses on the left. At the end of the road turn left and continue along to a bridleway sign on the right. Go straight down the bridleway with a hedge on the right to pass through a gate and straight ahead down a minor road. Approximately three quarters of a mile down the road, hidden away in a wooded valley in a bend of the Wear, stand the ruins of Finchale Priory, reached by either turning left along the road for a short distance before going down a series of winding steps to the right or paying one penny toll at the tiny shop and going down through the trees on a more natural winding path to the footbridge below. Either way the walker will be rewarded with a splendid view of the ruins which the visitors from the south are likely to miss.

At the priory turn right past the cafe and along a narrow road ignoring the turning to the left and the private path which goes down to the right, through a gate and along the tarmac road which is quite busy during summer weekends. At other times it is a pleasant walk with green fields to the left and woods and then an old army stores depot on the right. Turn left at the depot entrance and continue to the crossroads turning right along the road for a short distance before turning left down a lane where a bridleway sign indicates the way. The lane passes between the prison and the remand centre, a rather forbidding yet pleasant walk which soon breaks out into open country, crossing over the old railway formation where the crossing gate posts still stand and past some cottages on the left.

Along a narrow track through bushes the path soon opens out once again and the main line railway can be seen over to the right. Frankland Farm can be seen ahead and as one approaches it there is wonderful view of Durham Cathedral standing majestically on top of the hill dominating the city which surrounds it. The route from the farm to Durham needs little description, the track winding down the hill to the river and then swinging right through fields to the road which runs alongside the river and into the city. Thus ends the first section of the walk but if you wish for a really fitting climax, assuming of course that your legs will still carry you, go up those tortuous steps to the cathedral roof and you will be able to trace your route through the glorious countryside and, with a little help from a compass, the next stage of the walk.

Durham to Bishop Auckland

MANY people who walk the Weardale Way will have already visited and explored the City of Durham before but to those who have not I would suggest that their schedule should allow plenty of time to look around this exciting and picturesque place. It is of course impossible to describe in this small guide the city and its magnificent cathedral for many volumes have and will continue to be written without exhausting the subject. Suffice to say that the city owes its fame largely to the monks of Lindisfarne who, when in danger from the marauding Danes in 875, took upon themselves the task of transporting the body of their bishop St. Cuthbert to safety. More than one hundred years later, having bourne the saintly remains to Melrose in Scotland, Crayke in Yorkshire and of course Chester-le-Street and Ripon, the devoted band — now of course a completely different group, the originals having all departed this life — brought the saint's body to its final resting place on the heights above the River Wear. They then built a church of wattled boughs over it before replacing it as soon as possible by one of stone which over the centuries has developed to the magnificent building we see to-day.

Across in the north-west corner of Palace Green stands Durham Castle, the bishop's residence or fortress from 1072 until the foundation of the university in 1831 and now the home of University College. The castle comprises buildings of different dates forming a courtyard which is reached through a battlemented gateway. It was from here during this period that all the land between Tyne and Tees known as the Bishopric of Durham was governed. Space precludes reference to any more of the many buildings of note in this tiny island city were the surroundings are outstanding. Walkers will no doubt return to stroll along the narrow streets and gaze over the bridges at the tree-lined Wear with its delightful riverside paths which wind at the foot of the great promontory on which the cathedral and castle stand. Our route now lies along these tree-lined paths to Shincliffe where a look back will reveal the tower of the cathedral rising majestically above the trees.

Passing Shincliffe Hall, a university residence, the Way continues along a wooded path beside the river to Butterby Farm, beyond which we are able to stride quickly along the wide track to Croxdale Hall, for centuries the home of the Salvin family. A very imposing house with beautiful views across the parkland, it had a Roman Catholic chapel adjoining the house in addition to the tiny Norman Church of Sunderland Bridge which now stands deserted and unused behind the hall having been replaced by a 19th century building in the village about half a mile away.

The first task on leaving the path at Croxdale lies in crossing the busy A1 where the first of three bridges, a modern steel structure, carries the Great North Road across the River Wear. The second, a medieval stone bridge with four round arches, partly rebuilt in 1769 and widened in 1822 after a mail coach accident when two passengers were thrown over the parapet and killed. The third bridge, certainly the most impressive, is a short diatance away; the railway viaduct carrying the Edinburgh to London main line over the river is almost exactly 250 miles from King's Cross.

Our route goes under this remarkable piece of engineering and along a pleasant riverside path to Page Bank and the start of a walk through an area with the last remaining links with the local mining era. Little remains of the old colliery cottages at Page Bank although the evidence is unmistakable, but it amounts to a brief and almost insignificant intrusion into what is a pleasant walk to Sunnybrow, aptly named for it is here that we meet up with the first real climb on the route. At the top of the hill we find a very unusual memorial, a replica of a coal wagon standing on top of a concrete plinth which was erected in 1976 to commemorate the Rocking Strike of 1863, forerunner of the checkweigh system.

The way now lies along the formation of the old railway line which formerly connected Bishop Auckland with the main line at Durham, a walk of four miles where walkers can stride along and no doubt contemplate the splendid scenery which lies ahead as they enter the region known as "Weardale proper".

Route   14 miles

LEAVING Durham, no doubt regretfully, by the path which runs beneath the castle on the north bank of the river, under three road bridges and into open countryside, one can relax, enjoy the scenery and quickly establish a steady pace on the firm path. After a couple of miles the track goes across a meadow and over a bridge spanning a stream, turning left then right over the old railway formation and across the playing field to the river. Ignore the inviting footbridge, turn left along the river's edge and along a wide track towards the church at Shincliffe which can be seen directly ahead. At the river bridge turn left past the public house and the petrol station, turning right down a road, past some houses and along a pleasant country lane which is signposted to Shincliffe Hall. The lane gradually becomes steeper passing a nursery and a charming cottage called Old England, where there are splendid views of the surrounding countryside, and on past a private path going into the woods on the right, up to the hall.

At the hall, which is a part of Durham University, turn left into a wood and

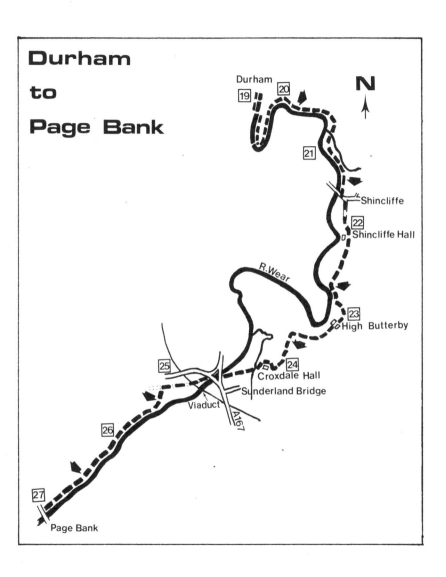

immediately right along the edge of it. The path now runs along the edge all the way to the river where it turns left along a splendid walk through the woods which flank the river, a little muddy in wet weather but easy to follow and providing some wonderful views through the trees. The path finishes at a stile near High Butterby Farm where our route passes in front of the farmhouse between farm buildings and straight ahead on a good wide track with a wood on the right. At this point walkers are reminded that they should keep to the right-of-way and not enter the buildings or interfere with machinery.

For the next two miles this track skirts the edge of the wood with pastures to the left and the occasional glimpse of the river snaking its way down below to the right. At the point where the wood ends one can see ahead the buildings surrounding Croxdale Hall and it isn't long before one turns a corner to find the wonderful little church hidden away behind a high stone wall. Pass the church and turn left across a triangle of grass and along the side of the hall gardens, over a cattle grid and along the drive, through the park to the entrance gates and the A1 beyond. Across the road and straight ahead is another road where we turn right and over the wonderful old river bridge, turning left along a wide track beside the river and under another magnificent structure, Croxdale Viaduct, which carries the main line railway. The track continues past a point where it almost meets the river to a kissing gate on the left approximately 400 yards beyond. Pass through the gate and go diagonally right across to the river bank, the path now continuing along the riverside for approximately 1½ miles to Page Bank, no doubt once a busy little mining community but now only a couple of houses remain. Across the bridge the old public house appears to have provided its last pint of ale a long time ago.

The path continues straight ahead along the riverside track, a two mile walk to a road bridge where there is a picnic site and toilets are available. Continue along the riverside path beyond the picnic site and along to a point where there is a wooden fence on the right. Beyond this and before a footbridge passing over the river look for a track with fence posts at either side going up the hill to the right. Go up the track to pass the distinctive replica of a pit wagon erected to commemorate the Rocking Strike of 1863, turning right just beyond it. Go along the road and after passing a stretch of grass go to the left over a stile and down to the old railway formation, turning left along it for the long straight walk into Bishop Auckland, only the public house in Hunwick Lane being likely to detract the walkers from their objective.

Bishop Auckland to Stanhope

WALKERS who stand and survey the scene from the old railway viaduct as they arrive at Bishop Auckland will see to the east, set on the edge of a steep bank above the Wear, Auckland Castle, a residence of successive Bishops of Durham since 1300. A battlemented gateway with a clock turret built in 1760 leads into the park from the market place and beside it stands the 17th century lodge which at one time was a woollen factory. The castle, providing many delightful walks along the tree-lined slopes and beside the River Gaunless and the Coundon Burn which wind through the park on their way to join the River Wear. Those who are fortunate enough to arrive on one of those special days when the castle is open to the public should certainly grasp the opportunity to look round this impressive building, the last of the 14 country seats formerly attached to the See of Durham, parts of which date from the 14th century. It contains some fine wood carving and a beautiful chapel with a 17th century roof having panels displaying heraldic arms which is said to be the best example of its period in England. A busy market town which has a long history, for the main thoroughfare, Newgate Street, was part of the Roman road from York to Hadrian's Wall, Bishop Auckland is now successfully moving away from the coal mining era, clearing the sub-standard terraces, improving the road system and greatly improving the image of the shopping centre.

Our next call along the Way is the village of Escomb, not by any stretch of imagination the prettiest village, in fact one could hardly find a worse setting for the little gem which stands in its midst. The ancient church, one of the oldest in England, is thought to date from the 7th century, and although there are several older this is the only one which remains almost exactly as it was when the Saxons worshipped there. This small, austere building, furnished with little more than an altar, modern pews and a Norman font, no doubt owe its state of preservation to the high wall and locked gate which prevents the local children making it into a playground.

However Escomb is a relatively beautiful place compared with the next village on the way, for Witton Park would be better avoided if it were not for the fact that there is really no alternative and the planners are at best making some progress towards eliminating the worst part of the village. But there are signs of better things to come for beyond the inevitable pigeon coops the countryside opens out and we can shake the dust of the mining villages from our boots and enjoy the views across the river towards Witton-le Wear. Before we reach there, however we skirt the grounds of Witton Castle, a 15th century structure now developed as a miniature holiday centre.

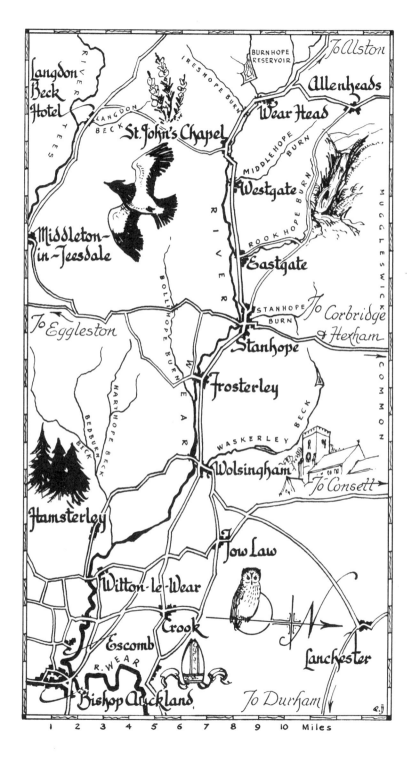

Beyond the river bridge lies a steep climb to the attractive village of Witton-le-Wear with its solid stone-built houses standing alongside an elongated village green with the church of St. Philip and St. James dominating the scene from the bank above. There has been a church there since Norman times but the present one is almost completely rebuilt with a few relics preserved from earlier buildings. The village also possesses two hostelries, both of which produce excellent lunch-time snacks, an important facility to remember when the next place for refreshment happens to be Frosterley some twelve miles away!

Beyond Witton-le-Wear our route takes us through the green pastures of lower Weardale with glimpses of the River Wear winding its way down below, the views getting more spectacular as we progress. Passing through Harperley park with the Police Training College over to the right, the Way swings round the impressive farmstead at Low Harperley and down to the site of the old station. Almost all evidence of the station has now gone but fortunately for us the link between it and the farms at the other side of the river remains, a footbridge, where no doubt many walkers will tarry alongside the sparkling waters of the River Wear. Perhaps they will stay a little longer if they have walked this way before and know of the climb up to the old quarry at Knitsley Fell which lies ahead. Beyond the quarry lies a couple of miles of walking beside the moorland road, at the end of which we find ourselves at the top of the hill looking down on the busy little town of Wolsingham, just over a mile away and 600 feet below, a handy place for those who wish to shorten this particular section for there are bus services, shops and refreshments available in the town.

For those who wish to continue the route now lies along the moorland track to the west with many excellent views over the moors to the north and to the north-west along the valley of the Wear. Beyond the elephant trees, so named because they resemble a pair of elephants when viewed from a distance, the Way turns down towards Frosterley passing Allotment House and Plantations, Allotment being the farm area between the permanent pasture and open fell which due to the poor soil and wetter conditions cannot be grazed as heavily as the lower pastures. It is also the last enclosed area before the unfenced moorland.

The Way goes down to White Kirkley, a pretty little hamlet on the Bollinhope Burn, a delightful stream with juniper and yew growing from the limestone crags above it. Frosterley, although not on the Way, is little more than half a mile from it and is well worth a visit even if only for the excitement of the search for the village church of St. Michael, built in 1869, which lies down little more than a cart track from the village street. Frosterley is famous for its marble which was quarried here and was used for church memorials, fonts, effigies, etc., throughout the world. There is a small marble plaque on the north wall of the church, the inscription below proclaiming this fact.

It is little more than two and a half miles from here to Stanhope, a pleasant walk passing disused quarries and across meadow to this old town known as the capital of Weardale.

Route   20 miles

RETURN to the river bridge where the last section of the walk finished, turning left just before it along a path which swings away from the river and alongside some allotments. Eventually this pleasant path finishes at a gate before the river continuing through it and round a bend in the river, through a mass of brambles and gorse bushes which take a bit of threading through at the best of times and can be very difficult to negotiate when the path is muddy. About half way a footpath sign directs the way to Escomb but this should not be relied upon for when last seen it had been badly vandalised, the next move will no doubt result in it taking up a position on the river bed! Passing round the bend the path becomes more attractive, running beside the river through meadows and over stiles towards the village of Escomb which can be seen ahead. Just over a stile ignore the path which veers left past some huts and keep straight ahead with a small hill on the left, over a stile and turn left into the village along a wide track.

Very few walkers will resist the temptation to take a look at the ancient church and assuming that you have done so, turn right after leaving it, past the Saxon public house on the left and shops on the right straight ahead along Saxon Grove. Continue on a wider track with a wire fence and allotments on the right, passing over two stiles and then veer slightly right to pass over stream and stile. Go up a hill to a stile at the top and straight ahead to another stile and a wide track going straight toward the railway sidings. Keep on this track, over the sidings and under a bridge carrying the railway and into what remains of the village of Witton Park.

Turn right immediately after the first block of houses and continue past the boarded up church on the right, turning right at the end of the road to join up with another road and alongside the railway to escape from this depressing place as quickly as possible. Approximately 400 yards down the road turn left through a gate and follow the track which swings right and then left along the edge of a wood to another stile. Go over the stile and keep straight ahead, ignoring a track which goes to the left, over another stile and down to the river. Straight ahead you will see a deserted farmhouse and a stream barring the way. Cross the stream and turn immediately left away from the river and just inside the wood where there is a clear track along the edge of it. This path ends at a wide track where one turns right, ignoring a track off to the right where there is a no trespass notice, and continues round the edge of Witton park. Over the bridge spanning a stream with a delightful waterfall, the track swings right and out onto the road at the lodge.

The route continues over the river bridge, veering left almost immediately

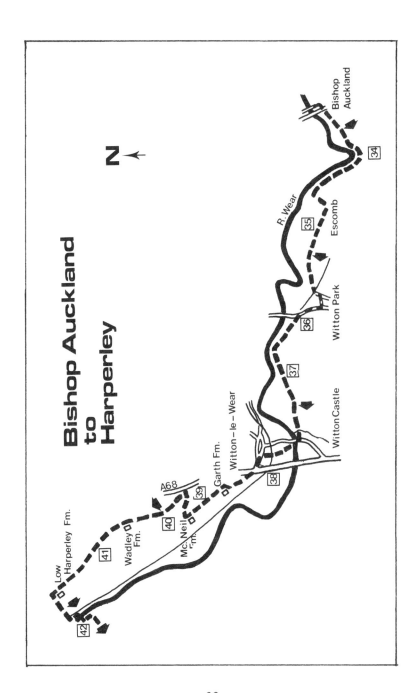

across the caravan park, past the Lido Cafe now derelict and turning right to pass through a stile going across the field, over another stile and turning right towards the railway line. Stiles and wooden steps will guide you over the railway and a stiff climb straight ahead will find you emerging into the village at the most appropriate place, opposite the *Dun Cow*! It should be noted that Witton-le-Wear is the only village before Stanhope so that any temptation to press on should be tempered by the thought that food and drink will be available when the pub opens!

Leave Witton-le-Wear westward or to make it simpler face the *Dun Cow* and turn left, cross the A68 and go up a grassy bank at the end of the bridge, turning left down a driveway where a footpath sign is hidden away. Turn right through a gate and ahead to a stile beyond which the path swings right to a farm. Pass over a stile and pass to the right of the farm before turning left through a gate. Keep straight ahead through a gateway and with a hedge on the right continue over a fence, through a gate and with hedge now on left continue to farm. Pass through the gate near the farmhouse and turn right along a good track which climbs rather steeply to the road. Turn to the left through a gate a few yards from the road and follow a track which goes to the right of a wood and then to the left of another one. Where the track swings sharply left go straight ahead to a gate; through it continue in the same direction down to Wadley Beck and alongside it to the access road to Wadley Farm.

Turn left and pass to the front of the farmhouse and straight ahead to a stile and a path through the wood ahead. Emerging from the wood go straight ahead across a meadow to a gate and on to a wide track. At this point Harperley Hall, the police training college, can be seen to the right. The track continues straight ahead and a farm can be seen directly ahead amongst the trees. Go past the front of the farmhouse, through a gate and turn left down a path to the old railway station. Turn left and over the footbridge spanning this splendid stretch of the Wear, no doubt stopping for a breather and a moment to enjoy the view before continuing over the bridge and stile to be found at the other side. Over the stile keep the hedge on the right, under a telephone line and through a gate continuing up the hill. Go up the hill on a clear track and continue to a cattle grid. Just before the grid go straight ahead and through the left-hand side gate. Through the gate turn left and veer across the field, through a gate and continue in same direction through another gate and to left of farm to follow the access road to the Hamsterley road beyond. Continue to the moorland road over Knitsley Fell turning right along it for an exhilerating two mile walk with splendid views over Wolsingham and along Weardale.

Ignore the first turning to the left and turn left up a walled track where the road takes a sharp turn right. Go along this walled track ignoring the one which goes up to the left and continue to Harthope Farm where the track continues on the open moor. Keep straight on towards a group of trees which can be seen ahead, known to the locals as the elephant trees because of their remarkable resemblance to a pair of elephants. Continue past them until Allotment House can be seen down the hill to the right and go through the obvious gate on the right and down the good track to the building, passing to the right of it, through a

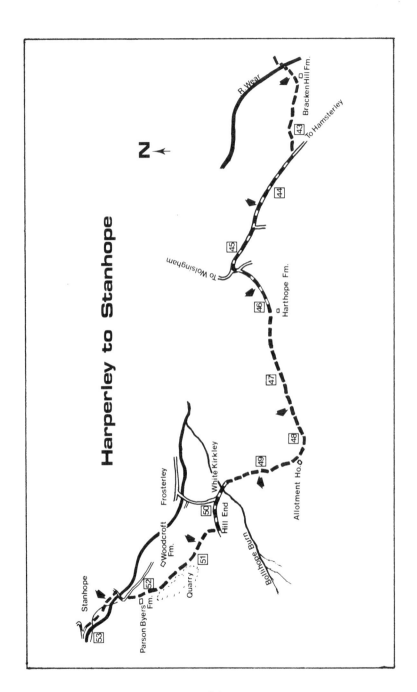

gate and down the hill to the hamlet of White Kirkley. Pass over the bridge spanning the Bollinhope Burn and turn left up the steep hill to Hill End.

At a footpath sign turn right through a gate and down a good trck which swings left beyond another gate and down to pass to left of farmhouse. Go through a gate and turn half right to follow a row of power lines turning left through a gate and over a bridge spanning a stream. Continue alongside the stream through a gate and two stiles to swing slightly right up to a fence on the north side of a quarry. Continue alongside the quarry within the field boundary and over a step stile. Veer right across the field, over a stream and keep the same direction through two gates to pass to the right of a farm. Go through a small gate and veer right following power line to a stile and turn left along road beyond. Turn right across the railway and river and then left through a series of stiles and kissing gates painted white, passing over the railway twice and along a lane into Stanhope, an ideal place to finish a section of the walk.

Stanhope to St. John's Chapel

STANHOPE is famous for the Heathery Burn Cave, scene of one of the most important Bronze Age discoveries ever made in this country. The cave was in the side of the ravine which is reached along a path through Stanhope Dene to the west of the town and which winds up through a delightful wooded gorge for approximately one mile to reach the Heathery Burn, a tiny tributary of the Stanhope Stream. Between 1843, when the entrance to the cave was destroyed during the building of a tramway to serve a limestone quarry, and 1872, when the quarry was finally abandoned, many outstanding finds were made which represented the complete possessions of a Bronze Age family. The collection containing spearheads, axes, gold armlet and ring, tools and kitchen utensils is now preserved as the Heathery Burn Collection in the British Museum.

The ancient town has however managed to retain some of its treasures. Possibly the one which attracts most attention stands in the church wall, a remarkable fossilised tree stump 250 million years old which was found high on the moors near Edmundbyers Cross.

The fine parish church of St. Thomas known as "the Cathedral of the Dale" dates from early 13th century and contains many ancient relics. The west window contains some well preserved medieval glass and in the vestry is a Roman altar found in 1747 on Bollinhope Common, four miles south of the town. It bears an inscription detailing that it was erected by Caius Tetuis Micianus to commemorate the capture of a bear of enormous size and dedicated to Silvanus, the god of the woods, who was worshipped by the hunters.

Opposite the church is the market place with its cross set on four old steps and on the south side the battlemented wall of Stanhope Castle, built in 1798 on the site of a former medieval castle. For those who wish to have a stroll there is a map detailing the local walks beside the bus stop.

Our way continues along a delightful path twixt railway and river to Eastgate, dominated by the 304 foot chimney of the cement works. A tiny attractive village, it also has its Roman altar dedicated to the God Silvanus, although in this case the villagers must be satisfied with a replica beside the main road, the original being in the safe keeping of Durham University. The church of All Saints is a handsome Victorian building with a massive font of Frosterley marble. Obviously built in an age when the planners believed in the future of the dale and an upsurge in christianity, it has a seating capacity for

every single one of the villagers plus a couple of dozen guests!

Eastgate was the eastern entrance to the Old Park, a former hunting ground of the Bishops of Durham, some 200 deer being kept in the upper part of the park. Our route now takes us up into the hills to the north alongside the Rookhope Burn, the first contact with this splendid stream being a wonderful view of the Low Linn Falls where the burn rushes over the rocks in a spectacular horseshoe cascade. It is the first of a whole series of falls, Dunter Linn, Middle Linn and Holm Linn, which make the walk up to Heights Pasture a real delight, despite difficulty at times negotiating the path which becomes very slippery after heavy rain.

The steep climb to Heights Pasture rewarded by splendid views along and across the valley, our route now wends its way through the remains of mines and quarries long since abandoned to Westgate, the western gate of the Old Park. The village is not very attractive but does have the advantages of a hostelry which provides lunch-time snacks and a shop. The surrounding countryside however is a different matter; our walk takes us into Slitts Wood where the moss-covered rocks rise vertically on both sides of the Middlehope Burn cascading down alongside the footpath. Botanists, ornithologists and geologists will all find this a place to linger and enjoy to the full before the walk along a walled track on the spring line of the valley, down into St. John's Chapel and no doubt for many a night's rest and an opportunity to prepare for the journey to come into the wild mountain region where the boundaries of Durham and Northumberland meet.

Route   **12 miles**

WALK out of Stanhope past the castle grounds taking the first turn left and then turn right just before the river bridge along a track passing between Quarry and river. Continue along this very good track to a step stile, passing over it and the railway beyond and continue over another stile and beyond it a stretch of the finest riverside scenery to be seen along the way. The path wends its way through the trees between river and railway with clumps of gorse providing a fine golden display during the flowering season. Before reaching the end of this stretch the huge chimney of the cement works will be seen directly ahead, the first sign of the industry which now dominates this part of the valley. At a caravan site the path goes straight ahead through a gate with a wall on left to a stile, turning right along the road past the old station. At the end of the road turn left into the village of Eastgate, where just before the cottages on the left-hand side of the road will be found a replica of the Roman altar which was found near Rookhope Burn between Dunter Linn and Low Linn in 1869.

For those requiring refreshment the inn is a little further along the road but the way lies along the lane to the right towards the church. For those who wish to have a quick look at the waterfalls, turn left past some cottages opposite the church and round the back of some buildings at a footpath sign to a footbridge over the Burn. Our route however lies straight ahead along a lane passing to the left of a house and on to Hole House Farm where the Way passes through a gate straight ahead and up a grassy slope through a wood. Through another gate the path passes along to a gateway where we take the lower track going straight ahead at a stone wall and two hawthorne trees and along a well defined path above the stream. The Way eventually passes beside a waterfall, over a small bridge and past derelict buildings to arrive at a stile and a bridge over the burn to the Rookhope road beyond. Turn right along the road to a tiny hamlet where you will find a footpath sign pointing down a path on the left with a stream to the right. Go down the path and then left alongside the cemetery, through a gate, turn right over a bridge, left and through the gate directly ahead, turn right then very quickly left through another gate and follow a line of trees swinging slightly up to the right. A short distance before a wall turn right up the hill and keep the same direction to the top where there is a stile. Go over it and turn left along the old railway formation. The Way now follows the course of the railway for a little over one mile and a quarter passing the farm buildings at Smailsburn and then straight ahead to pass a derelict house beyond which the track swings slightly right to a gate.

Beyond the gate and where the track swings left, turn right off it and climb up the hill in a south-westerly direction to the left of a gully. As the top of the hill is approached an old railway box wagon can be seen with a gate beside it. Go through the gate and continue in the same direction down the fell and aim for a junction of two walls and at the bottom of the hill you will find the remains of an old bridge. Go over the stream at this point and follow a good grassy track to a stile over the wall ahead. Beyond the stile go straight ahead to a gate and continue along a well defined track which turns left through a gate and down a hill passing old mine workings, the track swinging right before Chester House and then left through a gate with the old quarry up to the right. At the bottom the track turns right passing a white cottage and out on to the road beyond. Turn left down the steep hill into Westgate if food or drink is required but if not only go two-thirds of the way down the hill and turn right down a track just before a large building dated 1791.

On down the track to the edge of Middlehope Burn and the beginning of another exciting walk which will provide the nature lover with a great deal of pleasure, the moss-covered rocks along both sides of the burn which dashes down the gill in a succession of small waterfalls a scene of splendour when the sun glints on the water and no doubt equally attractive in winter when frost and snow turn the gill into a tiny Switzerland. But back to the walk, take the track past High Mill up on the right and continue along the gill, over two footbridges and pass through some old mine workings before turning left at a walled track and over the ford. Continue straight ahead to a walled lane turning left along it for approximately one mile before turning right along a narrow road, past farms to a point where just before a bridleway sign pointing up a green lane to the right you

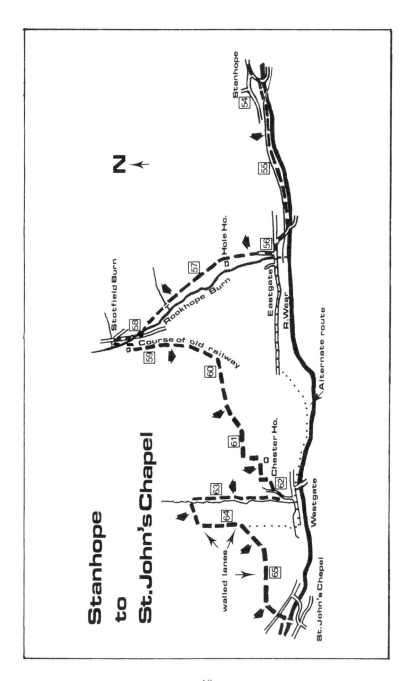

will find a stile on the left. Go through it and then aim for the west end of St. John's Chapel which can be seen ahead, passing through a couple more stiles and over the tiny river bridge into this busy little village and the end of yet one more section of the walk.

Alternative bad weather route from Eastgate to St. John's Chapel

The route between Eastgate and a point just west of Westgate has quite a few problems during bad weather; the burns are liable to flooding making the paths heavy and dangerous in places and the ford at the northern end of the walk from Westgate is not easy to cross in good weather and can be quite impossible when the stream is flooded. In addition the falls over Heights Pasture are not the best of places to be visiting when the weather is bad. It is recommended that the alternative route now described should be used whenever walkers are in doubt regarding the conditions beyond Eastgate.

Go past the inn and straight ahead for one mile turning left through a gate at the second footpath sign. Veer right down the riverside path and continue along it to Westgate. Turn right at the river bridge and then left along the village street past the inn and a shop on the right. Opposite the entrance to a caravan park turn right up a walled lane marked by a footpath sign. At some cottages swing left then right, through a gate and along a sunken track climbing up the hill and to the left of a building. Go through a gate and continue to the right of a house and to the left of another building to pass through a gate and rejoin the route by turning left along the walled track.

St. John's Chapel to Cowshill

ST. JOHN'S CHAPEL, the centre of activities in the northern end of the dale, is a small town with a character of its own. The chapel, the unique church of St. John, was founded in 1465 and replaced in 1752 by the existing building with its pyramid roof supported by four round columns. It overlooks a tiny green and the spacious market place behind which rises the 2,300 feet of Chapel Fell and Harthorpe Moor, across which the lonely moorland road links the village with Langdon Beck in Teesdale. The *King's Arms,* where snacks and evening meals are available, is also the headquarters of a little known Weardale organization. At the beginning of the 19th century the inhabitants of this lonely part of the world were becoming increasingly worried by the lawlessness in the valley and in 1820, some nine years before Sir Robert Peel set up the Metropolitan Police Force, formed the Weardale Association for the prosecution of felons. Should you be around the market place on the last Friday evening in May at 6 p.m., you will see the members of the Association going to attend their annual meeting in the inn, no doubt still putting Weardale to rights over a pint of ale! Should anyone think this may not be a serious matter, failure to attend a meeting brings an automatic 2s. 6d. fine regardless of the excuse.

It is only a little over two miles from St. John's Chapel to Wearhead. There are more adventurous ways of getting there but having followed the course of the Wear all the way from the sea it seems far more appropriate to complete our association with the river by taking a gentle stroll through the meadows and riverside paths. The river of course is now little more than a very attractive stream, the water clear and inviting, splashing over the rocks wherever it gets the chance to plunge to lower levels and completely different to the murky waters at Monkwearmouth.

The other noticeable change is the number of small hamlets in this two mile stretch of the river and a corresponding increase in the number of local people likely to be met. No doubt the explanation for this lies in the inhospitable lands to north and south and the even more desolate area confronting us to the west which would tend to force the old mining communities into the shelter of the valley.

Wearhead, where our formal acquaintance with the Wear must end, is a friendly little place where you can be sure of a welcome. The village shop boasts a bench for those who wait for the bus or enjoy an ice cream in the sun and should there be ladies without a seat one of the proprietor's chairs is provided with the appropriate old-world charm.

At the western side of the bridge the Burnhope and Killhope Burns meet, although the former only arrives by kind permission of Burnhope Reservoir, a magnificent stretch of water covering 100 acres and holding 1,400 million gallons to provide five million gallons per day to Sunderland, South Shields and Jarrow.

For those who wish to visit the reservoir there is a very nice 2½ mile circular walk, but our journey continues along the Killhope Burn beyond Cowshill to the Killhope Wheel, a restored water wheel which used to operate the old Pack Lead Mill. Approximately two miles beyond the wheel the road rises to Killhope Cross, at 2,056 feet above sea level the highest stretch of main road in England. Beyond the mill however the Way turns northwards towards the Northumberland border and across Allenhead Common, bleak moorland country with magnificent views but no boundary stone to tell us that we have passed into Northumberland for a little spying mission to one of its outposts. The village of Allenheads and the *Allenheads Inn* provides our first and last chance to enjoy the hospitality of the county before turning southward towards the Durham boundary. The inn is 200 years old, built between 1770-1790 and formerly the home of Sir Thomas Wentworth. There is a weather vane which acts as a finial on the west end of the roof with his title, initials and the date 1790 pierced through the metal. The inn provides comfortable accommodationm, good home-cooked food and a warm welcome to walkers. Only two and a half miles of wonderful countryside separates the inn from the end of our walk at another pub, the *Cowshill Hotel,* where no doubt many glasses will be raised to the County of Durham and its glorious countryside.

Route 13 miles

THERE are quite a few paths from St. John's Chapel to Wearhead, but having followed the Wear all the way from the point at which it entered the sea it seems more appropriate that for the last few miles our route should follow the river, taking us through pleasant green meadows in a valley now dominated by the mountains ahead. Beyond Wearhead an opportunity occurs to have a final fling, for after visiting the Killhope Wheel the absence of a bus service necessitates either a return by the same route or a much more adventurous and fitting end to the walk, a circular tour taking us over desolate Middlehope Moor to the boundary of County Durham.

Leaving St. John's Chapel by the same bridge that you entered it, turn left through a series of kissing gates and stiles ending at a cottage. Go through a stile beside the house and through a small gate to regain the riverside path, ignoring a footbridge going over the river and continuing along a very pleasant walk along the river bank to a road bridge. Go over the road and continue along the river bank and under a bridge, keeping to the river's edge to the left of Blackdene

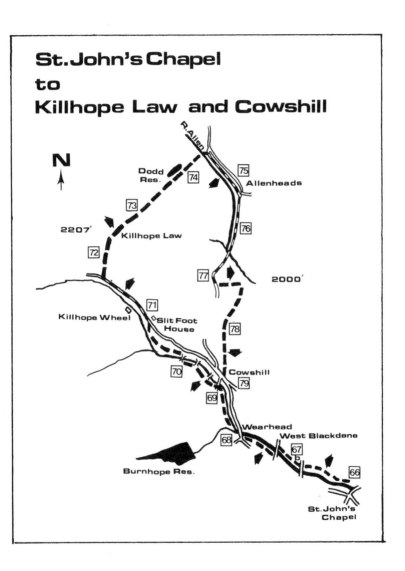

Mine. The path now runs between delightful waterfalls and pretty scenery on the left and the mine buildings on the right. The temptation will no doubt be to keep one's eyes to the left, but those who choose to look right will see two piles of very interesting minerals, fluorspar and lead, separated from the rock mined in the pit.

Turn left along the road at the very attractive cottages at West Blackdene, cross the bridge and turn right through a gate and then several more along the river bank to Wearhead, where just beyond the river bridge the Wear is born in the convergence of two mountain streams, the Burnhope and Killhope Burns. Both rise at about 2,000 feet and until 1930 both wound their way from the mountains freely, the former rising on Burnhope Moor and the latter up on the moors on the boundary of Durham and Cumbria. Whilst the Rockhope Burn continues undisturbed, in 1930 a huge reservoir was built across the Burnhope Burn completely obliterating the tiny hamlet of Burnhope. As there is only a right-of-way up to the edge of the reservoir our walk continues along the Rockhope Burn and the mountains ahead.

Go over the bridge, past the shop on the right and down over a bridge spanning the burn to the left, turning right along the side of the burn to a road bridge at Burtree Ford, a delightful little village just beneath Cowshill. Continue along the same bank of the burn past two more bridges and at the third one cross over the burn and continue along the other side, across the access road to Wellhope Farm and then strike across toward Slit Foot House which can be seen on the roadside to the right. Through a stile on the roadside turn left and go along the road for approximately half a mile to the Pack Level Mill dated 1860 but now better known as the site of the Killhope Wheel, a restored water wheel nearly 40 feet high which used to operate the mill machinery.

After visting the mine return to the road and turn left along it to a wood on the right where a wide firebreak goes up through the trees. Go up the track through the plantation at the top of which is a gate and beyond open moorland. Keep the same direction at first and then swing slightly right between Killhope Law (2,270 feet) on the left and a small hill on the right (2,050 feet). The path now meets a bridleway which goes to a shooting cabin over to the left. Continue straight along the bridleway past Dodd Reservoir on the left and maintain a north-easterly direction all the time to a bridge over the River Allen. Turn right over the bridge and right again along the road to the village of Allenheads, one of the outposts of Northumberland.

Take the Cowshill road out of the village and continue along it for approximately one and a half miles until the Northumberland-Durham boundary is reached. At this point turn left over a fence on the Northumberland side of the boundary wall. Continue alongside it for a little under half a mile before turning right southward along a track which eventually becomes walled and drops down into Cowshill and the end of this splendid walk across the County of Durham.

A few yards down the road to the left is the *Cowshill Hotel* — what better place to celebrate than at one of the county's most western inns? But for many the walk will not end there, for they will, like me, yearn to return to sample the hospitality and explore still further the wonderful countryside to be found within the County of Durham.